Preparing *for* Marriage

A Paradigm Shift

A book for young people before dating, courtship, and engagement

KUNLE AND WUMI AJAYI

authorHOUSE®

AuthorHouse™ UK
1663 Liberty Drive
Bloomington, IN 47403 USA
www.authorhouse.co.uk
Phone: 0800 047 8203 (Domestic TFN)
*   +44 1908 723714 (International)*

Scriptures marked NIV are taken from the NEW INTERNATIONAL VERSION (NIV):
Scripture taken from THE HOLY BIBLE, NEW
INTERNATIONAL VERSION ®. Copyright©
1973, 1978, 1984, 2011 by Biblica, Inc.™. Used by permission of Zondervan

Published by AuthorHouse 09/19/2018

ISBN: 978-1-5462-9549-5 (sc)
ISBN: 978-1-5462-9548-8 (hc)
ISBN: 978-1-5462-9550-1 (e)

Print information available on the last page.

Any people depicted in stock imagery provided by Getty Images are models,
and such images are being used for illustrative purposes only.
Certain stock imagery © Getty Images.

This book is printed on acid-free paper.

This book is a
Gift
To

....

From

....

Date

....

Note from the giver

....

....

....

....

....

Signature

DEDICATION

This book is dedicated to all young people who are looking forward to marriage and to all who continue to promote and protect marriage as an institution.

ACKNOWLEDGEMENT

We acknowledge the Triune God, the
author of marriage and of our faith.

Samuel and Shalom, our blessed children for your support,
contributions and being there as a sounding board for some
ideas. Our marriage mentors, Prof and Dr (Mrs) Oluwatosin,
the seed you nurtured over two decades ago is providing a shade
for others! Pastor (Mrs) Olaitan Adesiyan, for believing in us
and encouraging us to complete the writing of this book and for
Pleasant Adesiyan for your valuable ideas. Friends and family too
numerous to mention who have encouraged us along the way.

CONTENTS

FOREWORD

When my wife and I were invited to a Marriage Weekend in Nottingham, UK a few years ago by the writers, I had mixed feelings, primarily because of my work schedule at the time which left little room for family life. Thankfully, we made the right decision learning the Five Love Languages (Gary Chapman), danced our first salsa dance and took some ideas back to our church Couples' Ministry. We have continued to share notes in this key area of life: "… a man leaves his father and mother and is united to his wife, and they become one flesh." Genesis 2:24 (NIV)

Kunle is one of those privileged physicians who routinely look after two or more lives. He knows a thing or two about making adequate antenatal, labour and postnatal plans for the commencement of life on earth. Along with his wife Wumi, he makes a strong case for a paradigm shift in "Preparing for Marriage".

Marriage is a marathon, a union of two imperfect people who can only find perfection in Jesus Christ. Despite the opposition to God's laid down plan for marriage in Genesis Chapter 2 and the increasing divorce rates all over the world, we have an opportunity to rethink the way we prepare for marriage. The current fast-food style drive-through approach is a shortcut to marital disharmony.

This book leaves no one in doubt that there is no substitute for adequate preparation for marriage, starting from the home. Our conduct as parents is the relationship bible that our children are first exposed to, and in their formative years, the foundation stone laid for their future marriage.

The reader would quickly find answers to the "who, what, why, when, where and how" questions on building a foundation for marriage and I recommend this book to young people and adults alike.

Abiye Hector-Goma
Leeds, UK
2018

PREFACE

Marriage is one of the most important institutions and one of the oldest in our society. Many have experienced untold joy and comfort in marriage. Yet many authors have recognised the danger being faced by this all-important institution in our day and age.

Social media has brought the world together and blurred the traditional demarcation of the developmental stages of the young. Millennials are bombarded every minute with information over the internet. As a result, there is an increasing tendency to devote more time or to focus more on sensational news and celebrities' achievements rather than devote ample time to discover one's own individuality. Youth is a period to figure oneself out and learn how to be prepared to fit in and contribute to society. More often than not, attention is directed to education, vocational training, and entertainment. Less attention is paid to developing personal values that will sustain one through life.

As globalisation has brought prosperity to many, it has also brought untold hardship and challenges to individuals as well as the society at large. The institution of marriage has not been spared this blight. With globalisation comes diversity and juxtaposition of cultures and practices. Individual families adapt to changing demands. Some values are rightly done away with, while others are simply lost. Family support is not always there. Thus, many couples receive a wake-up call only when the trajectory of their marriage is far away from their desired haven.

Over the past decades, an increasing number of resources, in the form of books, seminars, couples retreats, and so on, have been directed at married couples. These efforts rightly focus on how to make marriage work and how married couples can benefit maximally from the potential locked in this heaven-on-earth institution. The joy of marriage, however, eludes many today. To a multitude of others, the joy of marriage is ephemeral. Many now wonder if it is not an illusion altogether. The rate of divorce continues to increase. The last time I checked at the Office of National Statistics in England, the divorce rate was about 50 per cent of married couples.

While many marriage books no doubt have been of great help to many couples, most of the issues causing marital disharmony are traceable to ignorance or lack of preparation. The situation is like that of medical practice. Over the centuries, medicine focused its effort solely on the cure of disease. It has only been over the past two centuries that humanity began to recognise the importance of health education, planning, and prevention of disease altogether.

We strongly believe that a solid education and thoughtful consideration of the important matters of marriage before entering into marriage would avert many of the calamities that counsellors often have to battle with. As the saying goes, 'Better is the physician that keep illnesses from us than the one who cures us.'

This books addresses preparation for marriage well before it is time to say 'I do'. The time to prepare is before individuals are beclouded by blinding love or besieged by the activities leading to the wedding day.

We are in no doubt of the blessedness of a happy marriage. God instituted marriage and blessed it. For the sceptic, the fact that the desire for a good marriage remains unabated and universal even in this generation is a testimony to its blessedness! Many long for it and most will have a go at it, but may the bountiful blessings be the readers' harvest.

We cannot afford to continue to do the same things and expect a different result. To fail to plan is to plan to fail. Most people understand this when it comes to passing examinations and preparing for careers. Wouldn't the same principle work if applied to planning for married life?

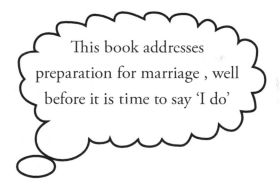

Why do we, the authors, feel strongly about this? Our involvement in the marriage ministry on two continents over the past twenty years has taught us that marriage is honourable and remains desirable. Most of the problems in marriage could be prevented with better preparation and good understanding. We have garnered over these years in our own marriage as well as in ministry, to many couples, important insight we could not afford to keep to ourselves. This has nurtured our passion for our children and the younger generation. We hope to enable them rediscover the immense blessedness of marriage, equip them with ideas that would help them plan for and achieve the best marriage could offer. Our desire to challenge the status quo is expressed in this book. It is our heartfelt prayer that the experience we have distilled here will have a positive impact on the lives of those who come in contact with it.

Who is this book written for? First and foremost, it is for single people who are interested in having stable and happy marriages. Second, it is for parents and those who have parental authority over the younger generation. As you read this book, freely work its teachings into parental training and advice. If all you do is to direct your wards and loved ones to the truth espoused herein, you will have 'acted well your part', in the words of Alexander Pope.

Third, we address youth workers and counsellors who find that questions on preparation for marriage are directed to them. This book may help raise topics to discuss and shed light on the path of those who come in contact with it. Last, to all who would come across the book—man, woman, young, old—we commend the book.

What is this book about? This book is a paradigm shift to preparation for happy married life. To become a professional, such as teacher, engineer, doctor, politician, or vicar, no one does it alone or by reading one textbook. Aspirants put in the preparation by following several well-designed, tried, and tested curricula in order to ensure they have the requisite knowledge of what the profession entails and demands.

However, during preparation for married life, most people never read a single book. Some attend a one-hour marriage preparatory course at the vicar's insistence. Others read the textbook of mum and dad, as providence would have it.

Who has ever heard of a doctor becoming qualified by reading only one textbook or observing only one doctor? Have you considered the fact that for society to allow you to drive a car, you need several weeks of instruction and training? What lies under the bonnet, how to check the engine oil level, how to handle the car, road signs, what to do if there are red lights on the dashboard, and how to recognize the signs of danger are only a few of the topics covered in the driving syllabus. You have to pass the driving test before you are licenced. All this tutelage and examination happens before you can drive a car!

When it comes to a spouse, on the other hand, many married people could not (metaphorically speaking) identify the ignition, hood, or fuel tank, let alone the exhaust, and yet they are licenced for life! No wonder some experience carnage instead of marriage. In fact, it is said that marriage is the only course where people are issued a certificate before they begin the course.

What if you could learn the basic principles of this all-important business before you get the certificate? What if you saw the certificate as a permit to continue to learn on the job?

...When it comes to a spouse, on the other hand, many married people could not (metaphorically speaking) identify the ignition, hood, or fuel tank, let alone the exhaust, and yet they are licenced for life! No wonder some experience carnage instead of marriage

HOW TO USE THIS BOOK

Please read this book carefully and use it as a template to explore what you really want for your marriage. We recommend that it be read several times. Repetition is the secret of learning. As Charles Haddon Spurgeon urged:

> Master those books you have. Read them thoroughly. Bathe in them until they saturate you. Read and reread them ... digest them. Let them go into your very self. Peruse a good book several times and make notes and analyses of it. A student will find that his mental constitution is more affected by one book thoroughly mastered than by twenty books he has merely skimmed. Little learning and much pride comes from hasty reading. Some men are disabled from thinking by their putting meditation away for the sake of much reading. In reading let your motto be 'much not many.'
>
> (CH Spurgeon. Lectures to my Students. Zondervan. 1979)

This book is intended to introduce the reader to simple but ageless truths. The reader is urged to discuss the issues raised with parents, guardians, or role models.

Parents are chief in the order of the most valuable assets we have as human beings. There was a time when each one of us were totally dependent on parents for survival. Even as we become increasingly independent, they are always there to help. Furthermore, two heads are better than one. We also strongly recommend discussion with like-minded friends and associates as you address issues raised in preparation for your married future.

If you find the book helpful, please pass it on as birthday presents, and make it available in your local churches, community libraries and sphere of influence generally. It is our heartfelt prayer that this book becomes a blessing to humanity.

Dr Olukunle and Mrs Adewumi Ajayi

CHAPTER 1

Can one really prepare for marriage?

-Kunle

Dream lofty dreams, and as you dream, so shall you become.
Your vision is the promise of what you shall at last unveil.

—John Ruskin

I will use a very personal story to illustrate my answer to the question 'Can one really prepare for marriage?' Growing up about four decades ago as the fifth son of my parents' seven children, I had plenty of time to dream—and by this, I mean daydream! I was blessed with a fantastic imagination. I dreamed of how I could do things better. I often wished angels would help with my share of household chores! If my daydreaming was interrupted, I promptly continued where I had left off once I was in my own company again. I often went over the dream several times in my head.

Although my parents were teachers, peasant farming was part of the children's upbringing. My brother called it a hobby. Not me—I hated it! At a tender age, I knew I did not want to become

1

a farmer when I grew up. I clearly remember occasions when I convinced myself that if I had only two options in life—peasant farming or grazing livestock—I would definitely choose the latter. I wanted more than what I could see around me. I imagined more comfort than I experienced. I gave a good deal of thought not only to what the future would hold, but with whom I would share that future as well as what I wanted my home to be like.

I have since discovered the truth in Eleanor Roosevelt's words, 'The future belongs to those who believe in the beauty of their dreams.'

In my early teens, I took up reading novels and stories which fired up my imagination even more. At one point I simply wanted to go to the university, ditch church, and become a university don so I could indulge my sensual appetite, or become a 'serial monogamist'* at the least. Easy principles were espoused in many of the novels that came my way. I was thus partly programmed to act out what had filled my inexperienced and naive mind. I was going to accomplish just that—but Jesus rescued me from my warped plan in the nick of time.

This is one of the reasons why we strongly advocate that parents should not leave their children to their own devices. Exposure to the devices and books may be inevitable but the parents should provide as much as possible a balanced view of the world to their children.

When I was at university studying medicine, about twenty-five years ago, I had a unique opportunity to join the fellowship of Christian students. My next-eldest brother, who had always been

---

* Eleanor Roosevelt Quotes. BrainyQuote.com, Xplore Inc, 2018. https://www. brainyquote.com/quotes/eleanor_roosevelt_100940, accessed July 25, 2018

a good role model for me, advised me to do it. I sought out the Christian union, joined them, and did whatever they asked me to do.

This was like the instruction Mary passed on to the water bearers at the wedding in Cana. It turned out, as the water turned into wine then, that my life took on a greater fulfilment than I imagined.

Among the many opportunities I came across were marriage seminars. There were a lot of them! I was a member of the counselling unit initially and then of the choristers so I found myself in attendance at most of these seminars. Respected and successful Christians were invited from different walks of life, especially the alumni of the Christian fellowship. What struck me most was how they fondly recounted their experiences while they were at university few years earlier, and how the teachings and preparations had benefitted them after they left.

The marriage seminars were eye-opening and instructive. They were down to earth and open. Participants shared from their successes and failures.

Preparing for married life had never been a topic of discussion while I was under my parents' care. I knew that the mothers' union at my local parish had discussions about homemaking, but topics such as marriage were not considered germane to the boys' brigade to which I belonged.

But in the Christian fellowship at university, the marriage seminars struck a chord with me. I soaked them all in and made efforts to read a lot about marriage. I also put in the prayer. Even if the prayer did not work, I reckoned, I had nothing to lose. After all, I was being educated. It definitely was better than ignorance. Now, as I write this twenty-five years on, I am glad I did.

These early experiences and godly guidance not only helped me in the choice of my life partner, they gave me the opportunity to look inwards and gave me some paradigm shifts, which in turn helped in decisions to prepare myself for marriage. This became the substratum upon which our marriage is built.

It also ignited my interest in marriage ministry and charitable works. For the past twenty years, I have been involved in different aspects of marriage ministry. I increasingly see the need to address the issue of preparation for married life.

When I was in medical school, we were told that it takes 5 per cent inspiration and 95 per cent perspiration to make it through. Once I heard that a few times, I knew I would make it through. I became a convert of preparing and working towards the desired end. I also figured that if I put the work into preparing for my future, including my marriage, I stood a higher chance of success. Once awakened to these truths, I dared to prepare for my married life.

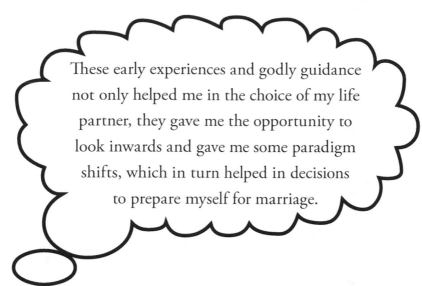

These early experiences and godly guidance not only helped me in the choice of my life partner, they gave me the opportunity to look inwards and gave me some paradigm shifts, which in turn helped in decisions to prepare myself for marriage.

My wife and I had similar experience during our higher education years.

In the past two decades of our involvement in marriage ministry, both with engaged couples and married couples, we have observed that most people were not prepared for what marriage sprang on them. Many were able to cope with the brutal surprise, but it is disheartening that some buckled under the burden. This is not to claim that our marriage has been blissfully perfect every moment of the way. That would not be true. But I am sure the foundation we had before marriage has been instrumental to the blessings we continue to experience at home now. In the same way, years of preparation in medical school and postgraduate medical training meant that I could cope better and even thrive despite the challenges that came my way as a specialist doctor.

During my university days, I had time to pray, to assess my priorities, and to consider what I wanted in a spouse. More importantly, I had the opportunity to consider what qualities I needed to bring to my marriage. I developed the qualities that would not only appeal to my spouse, but would make me a blessing to her. I had time to prepare my mind for few things that marriage could throw at me. These and other blessings garnered on the way, I have shared with the readers in this book.

Of note was dropping one of my standards. I learned from reading books on marriage that it was important to have expectations of what one desires in a spouse. One of my initial standards was that my spouse must be a university graduate. From a marriage seminar led by one of the senior brethren, a plastic surgeon, I learned that beyond my list, I should allow God to have his way. I had a conviction to drop that particular standard. Had I held on to my list, my wife would have been ruled out. Today, she is the pillar of our family, a blessing to us and many others—and a University Graduate!

There are many academies for ballet dancers, footballers, entrepreneurs, and ministers, but sadly, there are hardly any for marriage. It is common knowledge that keen interest in an endeavour and putting in the hard work usually lead people to success. Why should we not take such interest and put such work into planning for marriage?

To answer the first question in this book, therefore: yes, one can prepare for married life. I had the opportunity to do so. I am glad I did.

Chapter 1 Reflection

1. Can one prepare for marriage?

   _____

   _____

   _____

   _____

   _____

2. How prepared are you for marriage?

   _____

   _____

   _____

   _____

   _____

3. What preparation would you like to make for marriage?

   _____

   _____

   _____

   _____

   _____

4. Do you think one has a better chance of happy married life if one prepares well?

   _____

   _____

   _____

   _____

   _____

5. Give your own reason for the above answer:

_____

_____

_____

_____

_____

CHAPTER 2

Foundation Matters

-Wumi

It is not the beauty of a building you should look at; it's the construction of the foundation that will stand the test of time.

-David Allan Coe

'Poor foundation caused collapse....' This was the headline in the news following an inquiry into the cause of the collapse of a multi-storied building on the 8th December 2016 in Lodha Basthi, India that killed eleven people and injured two others. The report concluded that the building collapsed due to a weak supporting structure coupled with inadequate design and excessive load on column and foundation that caused sudden failure. The building foundation arrangement was said to be highly irregular and asymmetrical, leading to further instability[**]. This tragic story is just one of the instances where faulty foundations led

---

[**] http://timesofindia.indiatimes.com/articleshow/56396521. cms?utm_source=contentofinterest&utm_medium=text&utm_campaign=cppst

to the ultimate collapse of great edifices into mere rubbles. The importance of a solid / good foundation for a structure that will stand the test of time therefore cannot be overemphasised. No matter how beautiful a structure is, if built on a faulty foundation, it is a disaster waiting to happen!

Jesus, who is regarded as one of the quintessential teachers the world has seen had this to say on the subject of foundation:

> *"Therefore everyone who hears these words of mine and puts*
> *them into practice is like a wise man who built his house on*
> *the rock. The rain came down, the streams rose, and the*
> *winds blew and beat against that house; yet it did not fall,*
> *because it had its foundation on the rock.*
> *But everyone who hears these words of mine*
> *and does not put them into practice is*
> *like a foolish man who built his house on sand.*
> *The rain came down, the streams rose,*
> *and the winds blew and beat against that house,*
> *and it fell with a great crash."*
> Matthew 7:24-27 NIV

If we apply the same principle to marriage, the one with a weak foundation is more likely to collapse when the storms and the winds of life comes or when under a heavy load. Foundation is the natural or prepared ground or base on which some structure rests[***]. Experts would advise on the type of foundation based on

---

[***] Collins English Dictionary – Complete and Unabridged, 12th Edition 2014© HarperCollins Publishers

the structures that it is planned to support. A five storey building certainly needs stronger foundation compared to a bungalow. In the same vein, a man or woman, boy or girl who wants his or her marriage to weather the storms of life would pay careful attention to the foundation.

As in above passage, it is a matter of *when* the storms (the rain, the storms and the winds of life's challenges) assail not a matter of *if* the storm arise. Those who choose to build their house (marriage) on the rock are described as wise; those who do not are described as foolish. Life challenges are common to both.

An important part of having a solid foundation for marriage is deciding who to marry. Deciding who to spend the rest of your life with is one, if not the most, important decision anyone could ever make because it impacts greatly on how your life journey continues from the point of making that choice and how it ends. There are lots of books out there about making the choice of a life partner, knowing the will of God, hearing from God, etc. We always advise on this very popular scripture in the book of Proverbs:

> *Trust in the LORD with all your heart and lean not*
> *on your own understanding; in all your ways submit*
> *to him and he will make your paths straight.*
> Proverbs 3:5-6 (NIV)

Trusting in the LORD is simply about absolute dependence on Him and zero dependence on *you* or *your own understanding*. This, for some may mean unlearning the lessons that life has taught them that they can only depend on and trust in themselves. There are so many factors involved in the choice of who to marry that even when people profess to be 'trusting in the LORD' it could turn out to be mere profession and self- deception. It takes surrendering your will to God, acknowledging to Him that you are subject to error and cannot afford to lean on your own understanding and judgement, putting your senses and emotions under subjection to the authority of His word and being willing to accept His will even when it does not seem to match your expectations. God is a good father who has good plans for all his children and delights in guiding them. He only asks that we, through the exercise of the free- will he's given us, choose to trust him with *all* of our hearts and acknowledge him in *all* our ways.

I started praying about the choice of who to marry quite early and while I was training to become a nurse, I was attracted to a man that attended the same Christian fellowship with me. I went to pray about it and I was open to God about my feelings for him. I also sought that God would confirm one way or another if this was from him. I found out shortly after that that he was in fact already in a relationship. That settled it for me. I was good friends with my husband. I liked him as a friend but I was not attracted to him then. I also had quite a few reasons why he couldn't be 'the one'. It was a bit of a struggle to surrender my will to God's when I found out he is 'the one' after all but I have not regretted it! Surrendering my will to God also saved me from making a terrible choice mistake shortly after that.

It is important to note that God is not an author of confusion. He will not go against himself and his words, so it is important to check every leading with his words. It is also important to note that knowing the will of God is not a guarantee for a successful marriage. A successful marriage does not just happen. We have heard stories of couples with wonderful testimonies of how God brought them together and how they were meant to be for each other that ended in separation and divorce. Kunle would always say that if the marriage of Adam and Eve (despite Eve being created specially/specifically for Adam and the wedding conducted by God Himself) had problems, no other Christ- centred marriage is immune. How we nurture our marriage and handle our issues goes a long way to determine the outcome.

The illustration of a threefold cord is often used at wedding ceremonies. A three-fold cord is not easily broken.

> *Though one may be overpowered,*
> *two can defend themselves.*
> *A cord of three strands is not quickly broken*
> (Ecc 4:12 NIV)

The three-fold is interpreted as the man, the woman and God. God is the rock on which our lives, our marriage is built. Not only that, through the ages, men and women gone before us had this testimony of God's help in guiding their marriage. Forgiveness, commitment, sacrifice, trust, openness, faith, love, charity, and unity are amongst the most important ingredients that make up a strong marriage foundation. These are all ingrained in the Christian teachings.

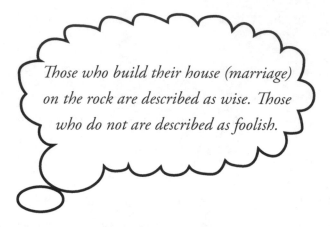

Those who build their house (marriage) on the rock are described as wise. Those who do not are described as foolish.

Therefore, in marriages where Christ is the foundation and the Bible is the guide, couples are more likely to withstand the storms of life.

In addition to the foundation, a well-planned house is supported by pillars. Such pillars of marriage in our own opinion and experience include: the body of Christ (the Church), like-minded and godly friends, family and mentors.

Finally, a great man once asked this pertinent question: *When the foundations are being destroyed, what can the righteous do?"* (Psalm 11:3 NIV). With a faulty foundation, it may be impossible to save even the most beautiful edifice of marriage. This chapter will not be complete if we do not consider instances where the foundations are destroyed through sloth, complacency, ignorance, stubbornness, lack of commitment, etc. We are in the days when people start planning for divorce even before marriage starts! There are people with contrary beliefs seeking to undermine or destroy the foundation of marriage. Some suggest that like animals, humans should mate indiscriminately, undermining the chastity of marriage. Imbibing some of these beliefs out of political correctness or for whatever other reason is seeking to destroy the foundation of marriage.

The other foundation that must not be destroyed is the foundation of faith. A couple must always remember the rock upon which their marriage is founded. The more a couple grow closer to God, the closer they will be, as God is like the top angle of their isosceles triangle.

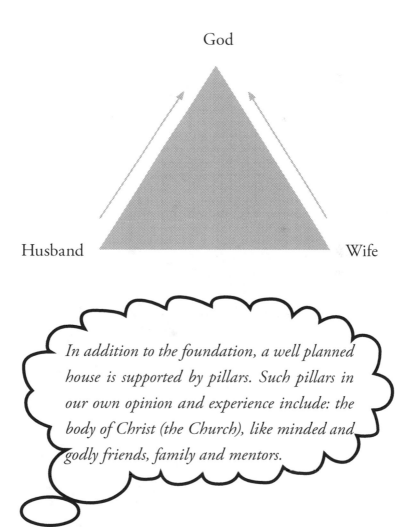

God

Husband Wife

In addition to the foundation, a well planned house is supported by pillars. Such pillars in our own opinion and experience include: the body of Christ (the Church), like minded and godly friends, family and mentors.

Chapter 2 Reflection

1. List 3 reasons why Foundation is important in marriage

_____

_____

_____

_____

_____

2. How can you maintain the integrity of the three fold cord?

_____

_____

_____

_____

_____

3. How do you plan to ensure a strong foundation for your marriage?

_____

_____

_____

_____

_____

CHAPTER 3

When is the optimal time to begin preparation?

Kids don't lack capacity, only teachers

Jim Rohn

We live in the United Kingdom of Great Britain, the greatest country on earth. There have been many enquiries lately into violence among young people, and we are amazed often at the debates in the media. Many criticize the government and her agencies for not being able to avert crises in society. Hardly is there mention of the role of parenting and family influence.

Most successful people are instructed, guided, and coached beginning very early in life. Parents are the first set of teachers in any child's life. Children need support and tutelage in order to develop their talents. Children learn by observation. Whether parents are aware or not, children learn from how parents relate to each other. The tensions, love, struggles, and triumphs of our relationships are assimilated by our children from a very early age.

Parents need to be aware that they are already teaching children a lot about marriage as they relate to one another day to day.

As adults, it's also important to realize that, unless we have learned from other sources as we grew up, our default setting in a marriage relationship is what we learned from our parents. Changing that setting requires a deliberate attempt to improve.

Parents and their children have been likened from ancient times to warrior and arrows respectively:

Like arrows in the hands of a warrior
are children born in one's youth (Ps. 127:4 NIV)

Unfortunately, many parents do not realise they are mighty. It is therefore doubly dangerous that the parents do not realise that their children are arrows in their hands. Some realise too late; by then, the mighty parents have aimed sharp arrows at their spouses by turning the hearts of their children against them.

Thus the arrows designed to be shot at the enemies of society, by virtue of careful instruction and living in righteousness, instead, become weapons to afflict their families and misdirected at their own married lives. *Misguided missiles in the hand of an ignorant warrior are indeed a double tragedy.*

It is imperative for parents to realise that, whether or not they intend to do so, they are teaching their children all the time about what marriage is. The standards are set in the children's minds. The training begins from birth. Thus, there is need to be purposeful in our relationships at home, in addition to providing explicit instruction on this all-important issue of marriage. When

we instruct children to compete, fight for their rights, and be helpful, or when we correct selfishness, disrespect, and ingratitude, we should remember that we are laying foundations for their future. Marriage is a very big part of that future.

Parents have a choice not to take simple things seriously. Nature abhors a vacuum. If parents slack in these areas, others—enthusiastic teachers, peers, or the system—will influence their children. I remember sitting with my son in a year five or six classroom (he was 10 years old) when the teachers were teaching sex education. I thought about how, as parents, if we don't introduce important topics at an early stage, it is easy for our children to acquire an unbalanced view of some things. It is even more important in these days, when an average child has the world's knowledge at their fingertips through the use of a mobile phone.

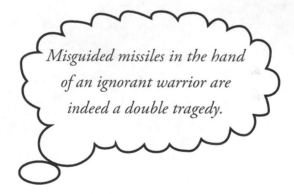

Misguided missiles in the hand of an ignorant warrior are indeed a double tragedy.

The basics of relationships should be taught to children primarily by parents and those with parental authority. Educationists are in agreement that there are waves of learning. Robert Kiyosaki, the author of *Rich Dad Poor Dad*, made clear his proposition that financial education early in life is important.

Children do not lack capacity; they only lack teachers. In fact most children are aware of or have acquired most of the skills they need for life by the age of eleven. Similarly, Warren Buffett, the so-called oracle of Omaha, is credited with the saying that most of the mathematics necessary to attain great wealth are taught in elementary school.

Furthermore, psychologists have demonstrated that our view of the world is formed early in life. We add that the Bible emphatically states that we should teach the child (not the adult) the way they should go, and when they grow up, they will not depart from that way.

We therefore submit that the optimal time to start preparing for marriage is in one's youth. It takes skilled parents to know what the curriculum should be. Many topics for that curriculum are covered in this book.

If you are a youngster reading this book, you have done well. This is the best time to start applying your heart to the principles that would brighten up your future. As young people prepare for their careers, this is the optimal time for consideration to be given to a bigger picture of what one wants in life. Beyond money and profession, marriage partners are extremely important.

The good news is that we always have an amazing capacity to learn and improve. Perhaps the reader did not have an opportunity earlier in life to study the principles discussed in this book. These principles are applicable and can be learned at any stage. They are proven to work. If you are starting at the age of 20 or 30 or even beyond, you still have all the requirements: a teachable heart and willingness to practice.

Chapter 3 Reflection

1. When should I start to prepare for my marriage?

   _____

   _____

   _____

   _____

   _____

2. What are the things I have learned from my parents and family about marriage that need to be emulated?

   _____

   _____

   _____

   _____

   _____

3. What are the things I have learned from my parents and family about marriage that need to be improved upon?

   _____

   _____

   _____

   _____

   _____

CHAPTER 4

What do I want my marriage to be like?

Begin with the end in mind.

—Stephen R. Covey

One of the most difficult questions one can ask oneself as an adult is this: What do I want for my life? As God would have it (call it providence or luck if you wish), our steps were ordered, and we pretty much had a good foundation for marriage. We were fortunate to have people who painted a picture of a good marriage for us in those undergraduate days. It was like beginning with the end in mind. We could not say the same for our profession, wishes for wealth, or other aspects of our life. Although we are applying the same principles to those other areas now. The words of Jessie B. Rittenhouse shed more light:

I bargained with Life for a penny,
And Life would pay no more,
However I begged at evening
When I counted my scanty store;

For Life is just an employer,
He gives you what you ask,
But once you have set the wages,
Why, you must bear the task.

I worked for a menial's hire,
Only to learn, dismayed,
That any wage I had asked of Life,
Life would have paid.[****]

This piece contains profound truth that is applicable to various facets of our lives. Progress in one's chosen profession, prosperity, marriage, and even health are often a function of one's bargaining with life. For the purpose of this book, we urge the reader to apply this principle to their married future.

The first step is the bargain with life. It is sad to say that many people do not know and have not taken time to decide what they want, let alone bargained for it. What would they bargain for? They have not carefully considered. Neither has it entered their minds that one could actually negotiate with life. They take whatever life throws at them.

The good news is that if you happen to be in this category, you

---

[****] https://www.goodreads.com/quotes/430858-i-bargained-with-life-for-a-penny-and-life-would

can see the light. If this is a light-bulb moment, then you still have time to bargain with life.

We have oft noticed that many people could not be bothered. They seem eerily content with the penny. Our prayer is that, if fortune brings this book to such a person, that person will please consider it carefully and give the principles a go. What have you got to lose? There is much to be gained.

Others, and we hope this includes you, have already started bargaining with life for a blissful marriage. Why would you settle for a penny? Why would you settle for a miserable marriage when life would freely give you a blissful one?

Consider what you want from your marriage. Consider what you want from your future. Then and only then can you bargain with life. It is this process that we sincerely want to kick-start in some and amplify in others.

In many fields of life, we are encouraged to write down what we want to do. In school, I was often assigned essays with topics like 'what I want to become when I grow up'. It is natural then to talk about a vocation or profession.

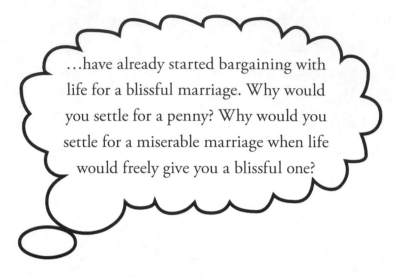

...have already started bargaining with life for a blissful marriage. Why would you settle for a penny? Why would you settle for a miserable marriage when life would freely give you a blissful one?

At this point, we are asking, dear reader, to consider and write down a few things you would like to have in your marriage. Think ahead five or ten years. Begin with the end in mind. Bargain with life for a blissful marriage.

Charles's Story

Charles was at the top of his profession. He met Sally fifteen years ago, and they fell madly in love. Both were doctors. They published a few papers together. Their publications were widely referenced by their colleagues.

Charles believed in evolution, but Sally believed in the God of creation. Their children used to go to church, but as they approached teenage years, they gravitated more towards their father's point of view. Of course it was also convenient to stay in bed till late on Sunday instead of going to Sunday school. This was a source of disharmony for the couple.

Sally brought up the topic one day. Charles, she said, 'Before we married, you promised not to hinder the children from being raised as Christians.'

Charles retorted, 'We never said we would force them to go to church. Let the children choose.'

'They are so young. We should guide them and show them the way. When they are older, they can decide,' Sally urged. She added under her breath regretfully, 'I should have chosen more wisely. Joint publication was more important to me then ...'

***

Stories similar to above are common in marriages. We are in no way proposing that preparation removes all troubles and challenges. There are some challenges that cannot be prepared for. However, the person who has prepared well is more likely to avoid problems from the beginning or during courtship.

Raising children in the church community was a priority for Sally. If she had settled in her mind early, Charles would not have made it to her 'eligible bachelors' list. If faith matters to you in that way, the time to settle it is before you make a commitment. If your priority is living abroad, living in the city, travelling the world, living close to family ... these considerations and many more are legitimate priorities. There are many otherwise-eligible partners who do not want these things. It helps if you know what you want and what you are not ready to compromise on.

Chapter 4 Reflection

Write down what you want your marriage to be like in the following areas.

1. Faith

    _____

    _____

    _____

    _____

    _____

2. Place to live

    _____

    _____

    _____

    _____

    _____

3. Spouses living together versus working away

    _____

    _____

    _____

    _____

    _____

4. Grandparents' role in your children's lives

_____

_____

_____

_____

_____

5. List other things that are important to you

_____

_____

_____

_____

_____

CHAPTER 5

What do I want in my future partner?

What has been will be again, what has been done will be done again; there is nothing new under the sun. Is there anything of which one can say, "Look! This is something new"? It was here already, long ago; it was here before our time.

Ecclesiastes 1:9-10 NIV

The best time to prepare for marriage is well before you have found Mr or Ms Perfect. One advantage of preparing for marriage before you choose your spouse is that you are free from all the emotional attachment and hormonal surges that could otherwise blindfold you. You can be more objective.

One should consider questions such as: What do I want in a spouse? How do I know that those things are the right qualities I should be after? Physical, psychological, social, and spiritual qualities are essential to the survival of marriages, and most of these qualities can be acquired, developed, adapted, and improved. Equally important is the knowledge that these qualities may change over time.

Despite great technological advancement in recent decades, human needs and desires have not changed much. The desires to be loved, cherished, respected, cared for, appreciated, encouraged, and supported have not changed. In fact these desires are much in demand to help individuals navigate the increasingly challenging world we have created.

Likewise, the need to feel we belong and are fulfilled in life has not changed. Human needs have played out in different ways among people who have long passed from this earth. It may do us good to learn about this aspect of their lives. Day in and day out, we hear or read about the struggles and challenges experienced by the rich and poor alike to find love, sustain it, and enjoy married life. Human needs simply have not changed.

The romantic verses so rapturously captured in the Song of Solomon in the Bible are a testimony to the age-old, God-given appetite for relationship. The opening lines provides us with a glimpse into the depths, heights, and delights of a good relationship:

> *Let him kiss me with the kisses of his mouth—*
> *for your love is more delightful than wine.*
> *Pleasing is the fragrance of your perfumes;*
> *your name is like perfume poured out.*
> *No wonder the young women love you!*
> *Take me away with you—let us hurry!*
> *Let the king bring me into his chambers.*

(S. of S. 1:2–4 NIV)

What do I want from my future partner? Abraham Maslow's

hierarchy of needs is a good place to start. This is an artificial stratification of human needs. Human needs are separated and ranked into five categories:

1. *Physiological needs.* These are the needs for survival, such as food, water, air, sex, and sleep. These needs are basic. The least you can expect in your marriage is to have your physiological needs met. Of note is that sex is placed here. Little wonder then that our attitudes about this three-letter word are important. It ranks with our need for air and water. But as basic as it is, it has the propensity to destroy a marriage if not handled well.

2. *Safety.* Security of body, health, family, and shelter fall into this category. Are these needs going to be fulfilled with my spouse? If these needs are not met, the marriage is headed for the rocks. Domestic violence, for instance, is a canker in modern society. It is no respecter of person, race, or creed. The onus is on any reader who has observed a tendency for violence in his or her behaviour to seek help and address this issue. It has the potential to bring a marriage down like the proverbial house of cards. Part of the preparation for marriage is to steer clear of people with abusive tendencies who will not ensure your physical and emotional safety and well-being in marriage.

3. *Belonging.* This category includes friendship, family, and sexual intimacy. Marriage is a marathon that goes on for years. Friendship, family support, and sexual intimacy are the oil that lubricates this complex machinery. A spouse with no fixed address, with no roots, who has no authority over him

or her could be a disaster. Often people need help beyond themselves to encourage them on in the journey of marriage. Would you describe your proposed spouse as loving? Are they a friend? Do they have family support? These are some questions you need to consider before making up your mind.

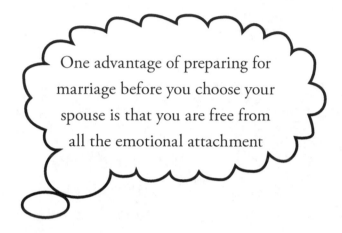

One advantage of preparing for marriage before you choose your spouse is that you are free from all the emotional attachment

4. *Esteem.* This category includes self-esteem, confidence, achievement, and respect from others. It is all right to start small. Most couples do. Equally important is to have vision and keep growing. Most couples would bear witness that respect at home and among peers is important. Does your proposed spouse have respect for you and others who are important to you? Would their lifestyle, decisions, visions, and aspirations accord you and your children the respect that you think is due and to which you look forward in marriage? Please note that this has nothing to do with possession. It is about the basic values we esteem.

5. *Self-actualisation.* This category includes creativity, morality, and problem-solving. This is a long term need. When the

fire of romance is burning low, when the children have left home, will you be proud of the person your spouse is? Can you look into the future and see your spouse helping you along every step towards your self-actualisation?

Maslow's Hierarchy of Needs

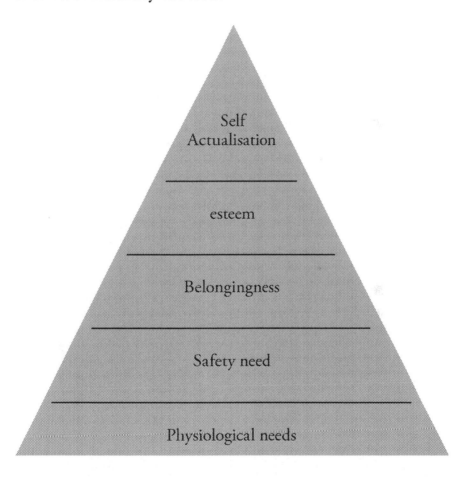

Self Actualisation

esteem

Belongingness

Safety need

Physiological needs

A representation of Maslow's Hierarchy of needs[*****]

[*****] http://www.rajivvij.com/wp-content/uploads/2008/09/Final-Maslow-1.jpg

It is important to bear in mind that life is not static. Our needs are often different from our wants, and both change with time.

A survey was carried out concerning what women want in men. It revealed that women aged 18 to 29 years were looking for beauty, passion, and illusion. Women aged 85 years and older wanted a man who was still breathing and who did not miss the toilet! (What every Woman wants in a Man, Diana Hagee. Charisma House. ISBN: 978-1-59979-059-6) Diana Hagee continues this theme in her book *What Every Woman Wants in a Man*. Women aged 30 to 39 years were wondering what they had gotten themselves into. Women aged 40 to 49 years were realising that what they feared at thirty had now come to pass. At ages 50 to 59, women had resigned themselves to the belief that their spouses would never change. Women aged 60 and above had learned to bring out the best in their men.

The young women who were looking for beauty, passion, and illusion have done well. These are only a few of the qualities needed in marriage. While they are important, the awareness that there are many more things to look out for would have meant less disillusion.

One sterling quality is faithfulness. The Bible states,

"Many claim to have unfailing love, but a faithful person who can find? "
(Proverbs 20:6 NIV)

This question should be pondered extensively before deciding to even consider looking for a spouse.

Like many situations in life, the results of this survey can be viewed in different ways. Pessimists will say '*Que sera sera*' and fold their hands. The optimists—and we do hope the reader is one—will see this as an opportunity to ponder and order their course.

Chapter 5 Reflection

Make a list of ten qualities or features you want in your spouse.

1. Physical qualities

   _____

   _____

   _____

   _____

   _____

2. Spiritual qualities

   _____

   _____

   _____

   _____

   _____

3. Indoor qualities

   _____

   _____

   _____

   _____

   _____

4. Outdoor qualities

_____

_____

_____

_____

_____

CHAPTER 6

What should I prepare for my marriage?

Without vision or purpose, the people fall.
The man without a purpose is like a ship without a rudder – a waif.

—Thomas Carlyle

Arm yourself with the knowledge of the purpose and essential principles of marriage. Thomas Carlyle is credited with the saying, 'The man without a purpose is like a ship without a rudder.' Ditto for a marriage without a purpose.

Often the vicar at wedding ceremony says, 'Marriage is instituted first for companionship, for procreation.' This part of the wedding ceremony is easy to gloss over, as most people have heard it several times.

What is the purpose of marriage? Surely anyone preparing for marriage should critically consider this. Failure to address this may turn out to be a costly oversight. When we look around us and observe how couples live their lives, it is easy to see the ones who have a purpose and the ones who have no clue. A resort to the Bible illustrates this point clearly. To the readers who do not agree with the Christian view of marriage, kindly bear with us and assume for now that this is true. After all, in lessons at school, we made lots of assumptions, such as that 'k' is a constant in mathematics.

Marriage was God's idea

Man is the crown of God's creation. Everything that man needed was created before man was. God then gave man the mandate to tend the garden.

The Bible record makes it crystal clear that God said it was not good for man to be alone, so God created a helpmeet for Adam. Adam was not the one who demanded or complained. God looked at the crown of his creation, and unlike in earlier verses where the Bible recorded that all was good, God said that it was not good for man to be alone. Bible scholars would therefore point out that first and foremost, marriage was for companionship.

The next question we urge the reader to consider is this: Do you need a companion? This should quickly be followed by: Are you ready to be someone's companion?

A *companion* is accompanying person, escort, fellow traveller. It has the synonyms *friend* and *mate*. Are you ready to be all these to your spouse? Do you have the qualities it takes to accomplish this companionship aspect of the marriage relationship?

Marriage is likened to a journey together. Whether the weather is fair or unfavourable, whether there are delays on the way or not, you are in it together. Spouses are meant to be companions. How disheartening is it for one to abandon their companion? This all too often happens in marriages when either or both spouses had little understanding, preparation, or resolution in their stance on companionship.

Next, it is not good for man to be alone. Loneliness is devastating. One of the worst punishments devised by man is imprisonment, and the worst possible form of imprisonment is isolation. That is a second imprisonment akin to the biblical description of a second death. Imprisonment isolates people from their companions and they become lonely.

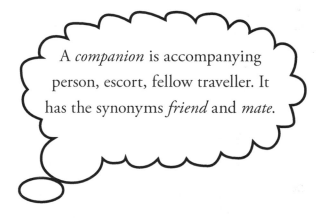

A *companion* is accompanying person, escort, fellow traveller. It has the synonyms *friend* and *mate*.

With this is mind, it makes sense that when God looked at the crown of his creation, he said that it was not good for man to be alone. Despite the proliferation and ubiquitous nature of mobile devices, many people are living in isolation and are very lonely these days. The Holy Writ has a lot to say about marriage and companionship.

In the book of Ecclesiastes, the question is asked, '…Can one be warm alone?' (Ecclesiastes 4:11 NIV). This could be interpreted to refer to physical, emotional, and spiritual warmth.

'If either of them falls down, one can help the other up. But pity anyone who falls and has no one to help them up.' (Ecc 4:10 NIV)

This verse refer to the second reason for marriage—to provide man with a helpmeet. Adam had an assignment to tend the garden. God decided that Adam needed help, and not just any help, like animals to plough the land. The help Adam needed transcended that. It was designer help, customised for Adam: helpmeet.

It is heart breaking to meet couples who are fighting with each other. If the only person who is meant to be your very important help in this life's journey is always at loggerheads with you, it is terrible. No wonder that people in such relationships are miserable.

A helpmeet is needed for more than physical work. Emotional help and spiritual help may be equally or even more important. Marriage should be a shelter from the storm of life. If a man or woman is maltreated or harassed outside the home, what a blessing to have a companion to go home to who is on your side, listens to you, and take sides with you, whether you are wrong, in the wrong or wronged! Such a companion helps you to make sense of things and just supports you. Alas, many a spouse finds the harassment at home worse than the onslaught outside. It should not be. Spouses are supposed to be helpmeets.

Another reason for marriage is the obvious one: it is for procreation. Needless to say, that does not only mean bringing children into the world. Otherwise, in these days of artificial insemination and in vitro fertilisation, there would be no need for a union. God and society are depending on the couple to bring up their children in the fear and admonition of the Lord; to be useful to themselves, their parents, and their communities; and to be a blessing to the world as they discover and fulfil their God-given purpose in life.

Many claim to have unfailing love, but a faithful person who can find? Ecc. 20: 6 NIV

It is better to live at the corner of the housetop than share a house with a quarelsome wife Ecc. 21:9 NIV

In Western culture, a lot of emphasis is laid on a fancy wedding and honeymoon. In the Indian subcontinent, there are wedding ceremonies that bring the families together for a week-long celebration. African marriage is noted for colourful displays and sometimes rivalry between the families of the bride and groom.

With the amount of time, energy, financial, and other resources invested in preparation for weddings, which many find exhausting, one wonders why there is hardly any place for emphasis on preparation for the marriage itself. We cannot help referring to Jesus, the greatest teacher who ever walked the earth. When he was sending his followers on a journey, he advised them not to take cloak or raiment. To me, that is like saying, 'It is not about the clothes, stupid.' In like manner, when he was commenting on the practices of the Jews, he said:

"…You give a tenth of your spices—mint, dill and cumin. But you have neglected the more important matters of the law— justice, mercy and faithfulness. You should have practiced the latter, without neglecting the former

(Matt 23:23NIV).

There is a tendency to join the crowd, to outdo the other person, to fulfil the dictates of the culture in which we find ourselves. It is not that these practices are unimportant. But while we fulfil this part, more attention should be paid to the more important aspect. So many thousands of years after Jesus spoke, it seems people still forget the weightier matters of life and marriage. All their attention is on the trivial.

Jesus concluded, 'You should have practiced the latter, without neglecting the former.' It is good to have a honeymoon and a great societal gathering at a wedding, for those who can afford it. It is highly commendable and recommended not to forget the weightier matters discussed in this chapter.

> With the amount of time, energy, financial, and other resources invested in preparation for weddings, which many find exhausting, one wonders why there is hardly any place for emphasis on preparation for the marriage itself.

It has never ceased to surprise us, when we get to address couples embroiled in marital imbroglio, that it is hardly ever a question of whether a spouse is good in bed. Many fights are related to sex, but not so much to the act itself. What matters is usually the relationship aspect. The act naturally follow once the faulty cog in the wheel of relationship is addressed, such as lack of romance or selfishness. The problem is usually other unmet needs, as depicted in Maslow's hierarchy of needs.

Willard F. Harley Jun. wrote a classic book on marriage, *His Needs, Her Needs*, after decades of involvement in marriage counselling. He identified two root causes of problems in marriage: failure to protect and failure to care.

Character traits

An important question to ask is, what am I planning to contribute to the marriage union? A good starting point is to identify character traits in yourself that are essential for the kind of marriage you are planning for. Identify the ones that need to be developed, those that need to be improved, and those that need to be jettisoned.

In life and in the ministry, we have interacted with a number of married and engaged couples and have also mediated in many marriages in trouble. Some striking themes—and the ones that usually baffle us—are character traits. They are the tell-tale signs. Many were there long before the couple met. These traits may never have been recognised by the person exhibiting them. Or such traits may have been identified and actively hidden early in the relationship. Traits are generally recognised by others, such as friends and families.

Character traits fall into desirable and less desirable categories. Desirable character traits include a caring attitude, friendly disposition, teachable heart, tolerance, patience, understanding, and ability to submit to authority. Negative or less desirable character traits include anger, lack of submission, and selfishness. (These lists are by no means exhaustive.)

Negative traits in themselves are not the major problem. We all know that as human beings, no one is perfect. The crux of the matter is that these traits should be identified by the individuals concerned, and measures should be taken to address them.

Can negative traits be corrected? Can desirable traits be cultivated? The following excerpt provides insight into habits, skills, and mindset: 'When the good king Saigon asked Arkad, in the book 'the Richest man in Babylon': "Tell me, Arkad, is there any secret to acquiring wealth? Can it be taught?" To which Arkad replied: "it is practical, your majesty. That which one man knows can be taught to others."' (The Richest Man in Babylon, by George S Clason.

Human minds are ingenious. People daily learn things they initially thought were impossible. We learn a lot of things because teachers, parents, and friends bid or influence us to do so. Once human beings set their minds at tasks, they often accomplish much. This include character traits, habits, graces, and etiquette. Once the veil of ignorance is taken away and replaced by the burning desire to achieve a goal, the rest is history.

The first step is the desire to change.

Some of the themes that have recurred in our interactions and surveys of married couples are discussed below. A wise reader will notice the one or few that apply to him or her. Blessed is that person who will make amends as a contribution to the glorious future they desire. There are books, classes, counsellors, mentors, and volunteers who can help you in these areas.

Negative traits in themselves are not the major problem. We all know that as human beings, no one is perfect. The crux of the matter is that these traits should be identified by the individuals concerned, and measures should be taken to address them.

Chapter 6 Reflection

1. Make a list of ten character traits you want in your marriage

   _____

   _____

   _____

   _____

   _____

2. List four of the above traits that you are presently lacking and need to develop

   _____

   _____

   _____

   _____

   _____

3. List four of the traits named in your response to item 1 that you need to improve upon

   _____

   _____

   _____

   _____

   _____

4. Make a list of character traits you now have that you need to change or do away with

_____

_____

_____

_____

_____

Essential principles of marriage

A man leaves his father and mother and is united to
his wife, and they become one flesh. Adam and his
wife were both naked, and they felt no shame.

—Genesis 2:24–25 NIV

Principles are very important in all facets of life. Principles are fundamental or general truths from which others are derived. For instance, the principles of aerodynamics guide and makes possible the safety of aeroplanes. In like manner, there are fundamental principles that guide marriage. The reader therefore will do well to be informed about and understand the principles of marriage:

- leaving and cleaving
- naked and unashamed
- one flesh, not twain

Leaving and cleaving

Anybody involved in marriage counselling would agree that many problems in marriage are traceable to struggles in understanding or applying the principle of leaving and cleaving. Scripture introduces the first principle of marriage aptly: 'That is why a man leaves his father and his mother and is united to his wife.' Genesis 2:24 NIV. The principle applies to the woman equally.

This short verse is pregnant with meaning. Six people are referred to. These six people have a great deal to do with marriage success. They are:

- the man
- his father
- his mother
- the wife
- her father
- her mother

The man and the woman each have a responsibility to leave their parents and cleave to one another. It is so disheartening to see men in relationships who yet are still tied to their mothers or fathers. To readers who are men, we pray you can see and have the strength to leave your father and mother.

What does it entail to leave your father and mother? First, it means a person going into marriage should have a degree of independence. This is mostly with regard to decision-making. It could also be with regard to finances and emotions. Although a situation may arise that warrants a couple living with one partner's parents temporarily, for the vast majority of couples this should be an exception and not the rule. Leaving your parents' house and establishing your own should be basic.

The onus is first on the man to leave. Parents, for various reasons, may be reluctant to let go of their children. Let the man considering marriage be informed: there are many decisions to be made which may not augur well for your parents but are better for your family. Independence is part of growing up. A couple going into marriage would do well to work on their independence from their parents as much as they deem reasonable.

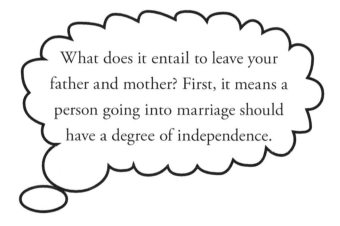

What does it entail to leave your father and mother? First, it means a person going into marriage should have a degree of independence.

One main responsibility of parents is to train their children from the time they are totally dependent to the time they are completely independent. It should be the joy of parents to train their children and be confident enough to proudly release them into the world. Then you can say, 'Go and show them what stuff you are made of! Go get them!' Like the arrow from the hand of the mighty, you will have no regrets in releasing them.

Naked and unashamed

'Naked and unashamed' means brutal openness and honesty. In order to enjoy and have a fulfilling sexual union (which is the topic of another book by the authors), most people would go naked most of the time. Hollywood has got that hyped up very much for the uninitiated.

Nakedness is a principle in marriage that goes beyond physical nakedness. Yet sexual union has much to tell us about the principle under consideration. Whether you remove the different layers of clothing yourself or your spouse helps you do it, you become nude, open, bare, even vulnerable when you become naked. Being naked connotes that you cannot hide anything.

You may have a lot you have kept well-hidden under the layers. The fact that those things are hidden does not mean you should deny their existence. There may be many scars—and the stories they tell. There may be lumps and bumps well tucked in that would be obvious if you were naked.

The Bible tells us that the first couple were not ashamed when naked. This speaks volumes. If you become naked to the person from whom you have hidden things, the sense of being found out is naturally accompanied by a feeling of guilt or shame. In marriage, we are supposed to be open, naked, and unashamed that our spouse is privy to whatever we hide from others.

If we expand this principle beyond the act of sexual union, the act of two becoming one and naked to each other in marriage applies to emotional, financial, and spiritual union. In all things, the couple needs to come off their high horses and reveal things they have kept hidden from others, perhaps for decades. Be seen as you truly are: stark naked. Be naked about your past, your hopes and aspirations, your fears, and your likes and dislikes.

Being naked does not mean you are in any way perfect. It means you are prepared and have resolved to work with your spouse without any sense of shame. This is fertile ground to learn to care for each other, look out for each other, protect each other, compensate for the weaknesses of each other, and be careful not to expose each other to outsiders—because you are privy to things no other person knows about your spouse.

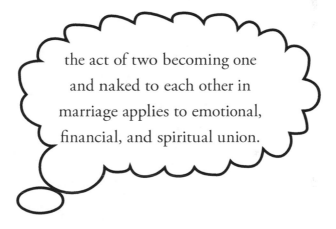

the act of two becoming one and naked to each other in marriage applies to emotional, financial, and spiritual union.

In addition, it is a position of privilege that your spouse has trusted you enough to become naked before you and with you. The reader will agree that any fortunate couple who understands this principle and puts it into practice are better placed to weather the storms life may bring their way.

One flesh, not twain

Consider these verses again: 'That is why a man leaves his father and mother and is united to his wife, and they become one flesh. Adam and his wife were both naked, and they felt no shame' (Gen. 2:24–25 NIV).

The reason that a man shall leave his father and mother is so that he shall cleave to his wife and they will become one flesh. To 'become one flesh' goes beyond physical sexual union. It is a perfect representation of the kind of union expected of married couples in purpose—financially, emotionally, and all. Being naked and unashamed is an important step. Becoming one flesh follows closely. For two people to be one is an amalgamation, if you will, that must take place.

Consider an alloy, which is a metal made up of two elements. Those elements are stronger together. Combined, their properties, advantages, and usefulness far outweigh their individual strengths.

Becoming one and not two, despite being raised by different parents or under different cultures, is a process. It takes time. It starts with recognising the need for the process, agreeing that it is possible, and then submitting to the process.

With the divorce rate reaching about 50 per cent of marriages, we are well aware that not all men or women will receive this message. we maintain, however, that if the principles espoused so far are considered, received, understood, accepted, and practiced, it is easy to foresee how a stable marriage can result. In addition, it is easy to see how difficult it would be for such couples to part ways. They would be so entwined that they would be inseparable.

We are not saying the process is easy. Nothing good comes easy. We are saying that it is supposed to be the expected standard and readers could start preparing their minds towards this desired haven.

It is sad to note that many couples do not enjoy even the most basic provision of their union—the sexual union—much less financial union, emotional union, and the rest. It is equally disheartening to see couples who will not consider holding their resources in common.

A few weeks after her wedding, a lady told one of us that she was keeping a private account to save money for a personal mortgage, in case of separation from her husband.

While that is the sad reality of our days, how we wish that the energy, cunningness, and ingenuity that is invested in making such plans were directed towards the weightier matter of marriage—no more twain but one!

> Consider an alloy, which is a metal made up of two elements. Those elements are stronger together. Combined, their properties, advantages, and usefulness far outweigh their individual strengths.

Our point here is not simply about joint accounts. It is that whether you have two accounts or ten, a married couple consists of two people who are increasingly becoming one, who have all things in common. All your resources should be pooled together. They are yours. You are one!

We again implore the reader to consider the many couples you are close to. Can you tell which of them are one flesh, which are in the process of achieving that state, and which are heading in opposite directions? The task is to look inward to see if you understand the principles of marriage. Does this understanding help you in preparing for the future?

It is easy to see how couples who have no understanding of the purpose and the basic principles of marriage end up fighting and turning the most important blessing in life into a curse. They turn a heaven-on-earth institution into a battlefield and the most important weapon to fight enemies into a weapon of self-destruction.

A pastor once said that couples who fight one another, unable to recognise themselves as being one, are like an autoimmune disease. In this enigmatic medical condition, some cells of the human body recognise other cells in the same body as foreign. The misguided cells deploy potent weapons against their fellow cells! It is self fighting self. That's why autoimmune diseases are so difficult to manage medically.

Chapter 7 Reflection

1. What do you think you could do to develop more independence from your parents?

   _____

   _____

   _____

   _____

   _____

2. In what ways do your think you could prepare yourself to cleave to your spouse after marriage?

   _____

   _____

   _____

   _____

   _____

3. What issues do you need to discuss with your proposed spouse before wedding?

   _____

   _____

   _____

   _____

   _____

4. How do you suppose couples can help each other to become increasingly one?

_____

_____

_____

_____

_____

CHAPTER 8

Know thyself

Kunle

Know yourself to improve yourself

Auguste Comte

This book is essentially about preparation for marriage. It is directed at those who want to have a fulfilling married life.

In chapter 3, we considered briefly the question of 'What do I want my marriage to be like?' You had the opportunity to write down ten things you want in a marriage. You can revisit the list, add to it, or delete from it as you deem fit.

In this chapter, we consider the qualities that will give you the kind of marriage you want. We then journey through self-examination. Lastly, we introduce some crucial principles that will help you attain, improve, and maintain those qualities that make for a fulfilling married life.

The essentials are these:

- know the standard you want in marriage
- know yourself

- devise plan to meet your standard

Know the standard you want in marriage

Growing up, we observe our parents, friends' parents, relatives, and neighbours. We often come across qualities we emulate or covet. Similarly, we come across character traits or behaviours we prefer to steer clear of. This is not new.

Consider some of the basic lessons my father passed on to me regarding marriage. While my father was growing up in a polygamous family (Grandpa had four wives), my father noticed the rivalry among the wives and the siblings. He concluded that this would not be good for the kind of family he wanted, so he made up his mind he would marry only one wife.

The reader may have no connection to the practice of polygamy, but there are other practices that you have observed in the couples around you. Perhaps you have observed domestic abuse, disrespect, or other things you consider to be vices. The decision-making process is the same as it was for my father. Make a decision not to follow in their steps.

Another lesson my father passed on to me: he observed (he had no access to books and instructional materials on marriage) that there was often a certain degree of tension between people who loved each other at the beginning of their married lives. Some were torn apart while their children were growing up. In some cases, the reason seemed to be that the spouses followed different faiths. As the children grew older, one parent wanted them to belong to one faith and the other wanted them to belong to another faith.

This, my father said, informed another of his standards: he wanted a wife who belonged to the same faith, and in fact the same denomination. While this may sound too simplistic for the present age, the principle helped him and benefitted us as his children.

This book is in no way prescriptive. It is intended to raise awareness in the reader of the little foxes that could spoil the vine of marriage and leave you in no doubt about the standard you could aspire to in marriage.

Qualities in my spouse

I desire a spouse who loves me, respects me, encourages me, supports me, helps me when needed, does not put me down, builds me up, does not nag or criticise me, brings out the best in me, forgives me if I wrong her, shares her life with me, is honest and open with me, treats me with respect when with others, is fun, is funny, shares same faith, and doesn't rebuff my advances.

For ease of understanding, one could divide these many qualities into categories:

- spiritual qualities
- physical qualities
- behavioural qualities

The list is yours; you may add or delete at will. A note of warning though. This is preparation. That does not mean that your spouse must have all these qualities. Life involves a lot of give and take.

Equally important, if not more important, are the qualities you want to bring to the marriage.

Qualities I want to bring to the marriage

After you have listed the qualities you want your spouse to have, the follow-up question is 'Have I got some or all of these?' For instance, you may want happiness, joy, and peace in your marriage. Are you a happy, joyous, and peaceful person?

Considering this question will give you an idea of what you should get ready for. If you want a peaceful home, then you should start thinking of how to pursue peace and ensure it. Conflicts are inevitable in marriage. A person who looks forward to a peaceful marriage must hone qualities that engender peace in the home. One must possess conflict-resolution skills and attitudes, and also must look out for warning signs of unruliness in prospective spouses. Even the Good Book advises:

> *Whoever of you loves life and desires to see many good days,*
> *keep your tongue from evil and your lips from telling lies.*
> *Turn from evil and do good; seek peace and pursue it.*
>
> Psalm 34:12-14 NIV

Know yourself

'Examine yourselves to see whether you are in the faith'.
(2 Corinthians 13:5 NIV)

You have considered the standards, qualities, and other things you hope and pray for in marriage. You have thought about these things with regard to your prospective spouse. The next task is knowing yourself. This is time for self-assessment.

The only assessments most people are familiar with are the ones used in the school system—the end-of-year or end-of-course assessment. This is summative assessment. It tells you whether you pass or fail and often compares you to your peers or a predetermined standard. Many have had the experience of being told they are not good enough in comparison to others.

The good news is that in real life, such assessments have little or no place. Another form of assessment that is more applicable to life is *formative assessment*. If we would but pause and consider how we learn best, most people would agree that first, through making efforts in trying to reach a set standard, we make mistakes. We try again by incorporating what we have learned during successive attempts and avoiding prior mistakes. Life does not issue you with a report card each time you attempt something. Each time a child attempts to walk and falls down, we do not shout or conclude that the child has failed to walk. It takes perseverance, help, and encouragement from parents and others to ensure the child learns to walk.

Thus, formative assessment is not a judgement of performance but a tool to help as you work towards a set standard. Knowing thyself will enable you to become aware of which qualities you already possess, and which qualities you lack and must cultivate.

I implore the reader to look inwards and see whether you possess the qualities that would contribute to the kind of marriage you have stated above. In the spirit of formative assessment, you are not judged or condemned. You are encouraged to look into how to develop the qualities you do not yet possess, improve the ones in short supply, hone the ones that are decaying, and develop in yourself the qualities that will ensure you achieve the kind of marriage you have always wanted.

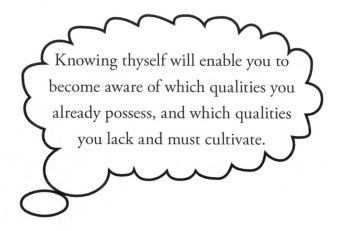

Knowing thyself will enable you to become aware of which qualities you already possess, and which qualities you lack and must cultivate.

Are the listed qualities present, in short supply, or lacking in me?

It is important to consider how to know if you have got the qualities above in yourself. If some of the essential qualities you have listed are absent or in short supply, find out why. Take it as a call to improve on these important qualities.

For instance, if I really want a neat house, I first must own up to the fact that I have not been a neat person. Instead of turning a blind eye, it would do me a lot of good to find out why I have not made effort to ensure a neat environment and then work on this.

The same principles go for whoever is not friendly, whoever finds that he is lazy, whoever is prone to fighting, and so on. One may not like the result of the initial self-assessment. It is good to remember that this is a *formative* self-assessment. You should not in any way be despondent or discouraged, because there are things you can do to ensure you reach your goal.

Beware of your blind spots

The Jo Hari Window

Known to self	Not known to self
Open	Blind Spot
Known to others	Known to others
Known to self	Known to self
Hidden	Unknown
Not known to others	Not known to others

I came across this very educational concept while I was studying for a master's degree programme in medical education at the University of Nottingham a few years ago. The principles made a lot of sense to me. They are used in education, psychology, and business, and are applicable in many areas of life.

The Jo-Hari window helps people better understand their relationships with themselves and others. It was created by psychologists Joseph Luft (1916–2014) and Harrington Ingham (1916–1995) in 1955.******

All your character traits have got to go into one of the boxes: open, hidden, blind spot, or unknown. Most traits are likely to fall into the open or hidden boxes. Yet there are some that will become manifest after marriage that are unknown to you or others now.

Open

'Open' describes characteristics that are known to the individual as well as to other people. For instance, you may know that you are hardworking, and others have acknowledged this. On the other hand, you may know that you are lazy, and other people are well aware of this.

The implications are many. If a character trait you consider essential in marriage is in the open box, you should not take it for granted. You should maintain it or hone it. If a less desirable characteristic is in the open box, it can be a red flag to others. It is advisable for you to acknowledge that characteristic, decide to work on it, and seek help.

Hidden

The 'hidden' box contains character traits the self is aware of but which have been kept hidden away from others. If you are selfish or afraid to share your true feelings, you may hide it from people for some time. But the nature of marriage relationship, with

****** https://en.wikipedia.org/wiki/Johari_window

the requirement that a couple be naked to each other, means one would not be able to keep these characteristics hidden for long. A spouse soon discovers, for instance, how selfish or self-centred their partner is.

Remedial action can still be taken after marriage, with spouses helping each other out. But a more excellent way to deal with such traits is to address them long before marriage, so you are in a better position when you commence the great journey. Of course, it takes openness even then to face up to those qualities. If these traits are not dealt with now, chances are that they will become open in marriage, and then you will feel that you have been found out.

Blind Spot

The blind spot is common to us all. Others see certain traits in us that we do not. Often these traits are flaws. For instance, if you are a go-getter, you may see that as a strength and be blind to the damage you do to the people you trample upon on your way to the trophy. The people close to you are the ones who observe these traits. It depends on the observer as to whether your eyes are opened to these flaws. It depends on your disposition as to whether you will be approachable, accepting, and willing to make changes.

This underscores the importance of others in our lives. We will look into mentoring, being subject to authority, and communication in later chapters. These help us to become aware of our blind spots. It is similar to car drivers: you depend on mirrors and, sometimes, the honking horns of other cars to see what's in your blind spot.

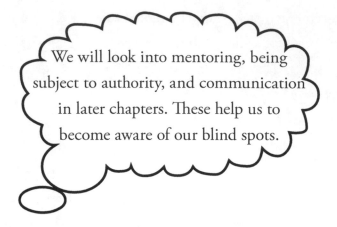

We will look into mentoring, being subject to authority, and communication in later chapters. These help us to become aware of our blind spots.

Unknown

These traits are unknown to you and to others. It may be that these traits will come to light after marriage. There is no way to know now. But the principles for dealing with these traits when they do come to light are the same: acknowledge them and work on them. If you deal with your identified undesirable characteristics now, before marriage, you will be in a far better position to deal with unknown traits that crop up later, during marriage.

Devise a plan to meet and maintain a standard

Most of the next chapters are devoted to steps that have been proven to succeed for people of various ages and in different fields of endeavour, in order to prepare you for the goals you set for yourself. Once you have decided what you want in a marriage, you have gained good insight into who you are. The principles we are about to consider in later chapters will thus be easy to adapt for yourself.

Chapter 8 Reflection

1. List five good qualities and five less desirable qualities you would place in your 'open' box

    _____

    _____

    _____

    _____

    _____

2. List five good qualities and five less desirable qualities you would place in your 'hidden' box

    _____

    _____

    _____

    _____

    _____

3. List five good qualities and five less desirable qualities you (or others) would place in your 'blind' box

    _____

    _____

    _____

    _____

    _____

4. How do you plan to deal with the less desirable traits or characters in yourself?

_____

_____

_____

_____

_____

CHAPTER 9

Train yourself

Kunle

As you make your bed, so you lie on it.

This saying is worth its weight in gold. How many times did parents drum this into their children's hearing? We continue to tell our children the same. We ask the reader to apply this to marriage matters. It is your life and you shall be the sole partaker of whatsoever you invest in.

Be interested. Take the bargain of life seriously. Jim Rohn puts it differently in his classic audio book, *The Art of Exceptional Living*:[*]

Tom: Come here and dig gold

John: I have no Shovel

---

[*] **Jim Rohn. The Art of Exceptional Living. Audio book. Simon and Schuster Audio**

Tom: Get thee one

John: Do you know how much they charge for a shovel?

You should not be John in this conversation. The invitation to deal with suboptimal character traits is akin to Tom's invitation. Please don't say you have no shovel! Don't put a price on what is required to develop the qualities that will bring you a fulfilled married life. Don't leave it to luck.

Train yourself. Cultivate good habits. Replace bad habits with great ones. It is called personal development. Effort is not only required in schoolwork or sports. We are required to apply our strength and intellect to acquire anything that is needful for us in life.

There is no doubt that a happy marriage is desirable and should be pursued. We have established that marriage was initiated by God and has brought heaven on earth to many. Yet it has and still brings untold sadness and sorrow to many others. The antidote is not inactivity and wishful thinking; it is purposeful and persistent preparation.

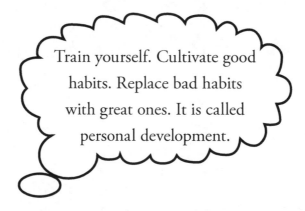

Here are some suggestions on ways to train yourself. These are ways that do not involve direct input from others. We will also discuss ways that involve other people.

Learn from your parents

Parents nurture their children and serve as the first teachers. Parents are often a lifelong support and help to their children. Parents teach as much as they choose. It behoves children to learn as much from their parents as they can.

I already alluded to the lessons my father learned from his parents. He learned to avoid the ills of polygamous marriage. Our parents may not be perfect, but often they teach excellent lessons about relationships. Sometimes the best lesson we learn is not to repeat our parents' mistakes. Learn not to justify the bad actions or behaviours, even if carried out by your beloved and respected parents.

The story is told of two children of an alcoholic father. One turned out to be an alcoholic and the other a teetotaller. The former claimed he became an alcoholic because that was all he ever learned of his father. The other claimed he learned never to touch alcohol because of what alcohol did to his father and family. Two students (children), one teacher (father), and two end results. The lesson is we can learn important lessons even from unlikely sources and challenging circumstances. Do learn all you can and decide to follow the best.

Observe and learn from other people

No man is an island. Many people, as they grow up, have other people they look up to or who exert influence on them. A story was told by a marriage counsellor, Mr Chan, of a young man who approached him. The young man asked to observe Mr Chan's family. The young man admired what he saw in Mr Chan's family and wanted his home to be like that in the near future.

What he saw in his parents' home was at variance with what obtained in Mr Chan's. He could have become cynical about Mr Chan's family. He could have decided to complain about and decry his misfortune. Some would even blame God for such perceived misfortune. Not this guy. He saw an opportunity to observe closely and improve tremendously in preparation for his later years.

We learn a lot by observing other people. Youngsters meet and interact with couples. Most will have a clear idea of which ones to emulate and which ones to steer clear of.

Reading books on marriage

'Knowledge is gold. Dig it.' This statement was etched on a dilapidated primary school wall in my district in Nigeria. I passed by it as a young doctor about ten years ago, and I wondered how true it is.

Reading books and thereby acquiring knowledge on the subject matter is one of the most tried and tested means to success in any human endeavour. I still remember some of the books I read on the subject before I started going out with my spouse. For instance I remember, Charles Haddon Spurgeon statement in John Ploughman's talks: 'They who join their love in God above, who pray to love, and love to pray, will find that love and joy will never cloy.' I have also never lost sight of sayings like 'The family who prays together stays together.'*********

Someone once told me that if you want to be wealthy, the number of books you have read on the subject should be at least equal to your age. I have since extended that principle to successful marriage. Once you read many books, a common theme will emerge, and you will have the important things to guide and help in your pursuit of happy married life.

Audio books

The technological age has made the acquisition of knowledge easier. Some use this as an excuse to wallow in mediocrity—who has time to read it all? Audio books are an excellent way to acquire knowledge in almost any subject of interest while in the car, in the garden, on the way to school or work, at the gym, and so on. Virtually at any time in any place, you could be drinking at the Pierian Spring.

By listening to this book on audio, you will need only a few hours to assimilate what we have carefully observed, handled, tried, and tested over the past four decades. This, we hope, will surely be a rich source of instruction on marriage.

********* *Charles H Spurgeon in John Plouhgman's Talks. Whitaker House*

Messages and lectures

A university don once told us that it takes three to six hours to prepare for a lecture he will deliver in an hour. Three hours plus years of experience was delivered to us in one hour. How precious that one hour was for us the students.

Advice on achieving a balanced life, like a balanced diet, suggests we should feed on varieties of 'food'. Using tapes, lectures, and messages as part of your education diet about marriage comes highly recommended as significant nutrient in preparing for the future.

Conference and Seminars

We were privileged to have attended many marriage seminars as university students. They exposed us to different approaches, thinking, and challenges inherent in marriage. We were inspired to find ways of continually improving our lives. They provided opportunities for us to establish our priorities, order them, and reorder them.

Several years on, we are very grateful to the brothers and sisters who thought it right to include those sessions in our developmental programme. We are still reaping the benefits today. We unreservedly recommend marriage seminars and conferences to all. Two decades on, we still attend marriage conferences and seminars for our own good.

Chapter 9 Reflection

1. List five books related to marriage that you plan to read

   _____

   _____

   _____

   _____

   _____

2. What would it take for you to attend a seminar or conference related to marriage yearly?

   _____

   _____

   _____

   _____

   _____

3. List five good qualities you learned from your parents about marriage

   _____

   _____

   _____

   _____

   _____

4. List five couples who have been examples to you in marriage

_____

_____

_____

_____

_____

CHAPTER 10

Allow others to help you: Mentoring

Mentoring is: Sharing Life's experiences

Janet Thompson

When we became engaged while at university, we approached a lovely couple, senior colleagues, to help and guide us along. We did not realise that was *mentoring* then. We just wanted a couple we admired to provide the guidance we needed as we considered courtship and marriage. To us, it was an uncharted territory.

Their mentoring was immensely beneficial to us. They invited us to their home, had discussions with us and gave us their insight. They prayed with us, asked about how we resolved our conflicts, and supported us. They simply mentored us.

More than two decades on, we remain eternally grateful to our mentors. I benefitted so much from them that we have sought out mentors in our professions as well.

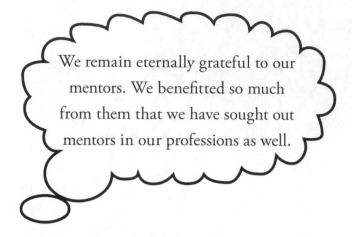

We remain eternally grateful to our mentors. We benefitted so much from them that we have sought out mentors in our professions as well.

A mentor is somebody who has been or is already where you want to be, and so can support you in various ways on your journey there. Mentoring is extremely important:

- see the need for mentoring
- allow mentors to do their job
- be mentored

See the need for mentoring

The authors have been privileged to be involved in supporting couples whose marriages are going through turbulent periods. We have discovered that some of the most difficult cases involve where either or both partners have nobody who could exercise authority over them. In such cases it is usually difficult to resolve the issues. In fact, it is our considered opinion that when a youngster has no one who is in a position of authority over him or her, it should be a warning sign not to go into a relationship with such. A person who has no one who exercises authority or constraint over him or her, in our view, is not a very good spouse material. Such a person is like a fine car without good brakes. What would happen to them when the character traits in the Jo-Hari 'unknown' box are revealed in their relationship? Who would call them to order?

Having a mentor is like standing on the shoulders of giants. Mentors provide advice and guidance; they benefit the mentee by making their experience and connections available.

Getting a mentor for your relationship should be a joint decision by the mentored couple. Mentors have reached the place where you aspire to be. The most important point is to consider your need for mentorship and to obtain mentors as soon as you are in a relationship that you hope will culminate in marriage.

Allow mentors to do their job

Benefitting maximally from mentorship is a form of learning. As there are many barriers to learning, so there are barriers to being mentored. Some people go to school and, for various reasons, do not get the best out of the opportunity. The same is possible for people who approach a mentor and do not heed the advice, take correction, or engage with the process.

Nobody should be compelled into a mentor-mentee relationship. Find one that is suitable for both of you. You may approach or try many mentors before you find a suitable one. But by all means do that work.

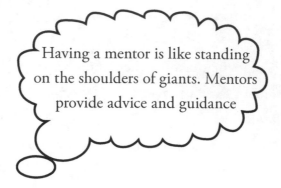

Having a mentor is like standing on the shoulders of giants. Mentors provide advice and guidance

Be mentored

Sometimes your views may be at variance with those of your mentor. This is an opportunity to consider the issue further or seek more information so you will be better informed.

Other times, mentors raise an issue you have never considered before. I remember clearly that our mentor when we were engaged asked us who would be washing our underpants when we were married. I wanted to blurt out, 'My wife, of course!' But on second thought, I refrained from answering. Just because I assumed that such washing up was a woman's job (my observation when I was growing up) did not mean it must always be so. On that fateful day, I had the opportunity to consider the matter in a new light. It was an opportunity to see my mentor's point, and I recalibrated in my mind.

This question by my mentor set me thinking. Here was I, in courtship, and I had never even given a thought to this simple question. I realised there must be myriads of questions that would arise in marriage later on that had never crossed my mind. It left me with the resolve to be open-minded, to refuse to be set in my ways, and to find out more about that all-important journey into marriage prayerfully.

Chapter 10 Reflection

1. List five people you know who you could approach to be your mentor in marriage matters

   _____

   _____

   _____

   _____

   _____

2. List ten things you would like to ask your mentor

   _____

   _____

   _____

   _____

   _____

CHAPTER 11

Allow God to help you

Kunle

"Let go of what you think you know. Something amazing happens when you let God and trust."

— Tammy L. Kubasko

The story is told of a wealthy man who employed a nanny to take care of his strong-willed child. As the man sat in his study, he heard the child crying loudly. He called the nanny and demanded the reason for the child's cry.

'Don't mind him, sir,' replied the nanny. 'He is crying for something he wants, and I am not willing to give it to him.'

'I demand that you give my child what he wants,' commanded the father.

The nanny protested, but the man would have none of it. Emboldened that the nanny had received a scolding, the boy had his way even before the nanny returned to the nursery.

Almost immediately after the conversation, another cry came

out from the child. This time it was much stronger and more intense. Irritated, the father walked menacingly towards the nanny and his son.

The nanny shouted at the top of her voice, 'He had taken it before I realised!' pre-empting the scolding she had experienced in the past.

'What in heaven's name did he want?' the father demanded.

'A wasp,' replied the nanny.

I liken the nanny in this story to God and his Word. His Word is a lamp unto our feet and a light unto our path. We are inclined to reach out for the wasp in our relationships. Things that sting us abound in the world around us. Like the child, most people have a wealthy and influential father in the form of the government or societal pressure.

Learn the simple lessons: this is your life, God's commands are not grievous, and millions of people have depended on those commands over the past millennia. You may then discover that the nanny is sensible. Stop crying to the father figure who has little or no understanding of what is happening at your end.

As a young boy, I read *The Power of Positive Thinking* by Dr Norman Vincent Peale. I came across the phrase 'Let go and let God.' I did not have much to let go anyway, so I tried letting go and letting God. I can confidently say that it was one of the best decisions of my life.

Oh, the storms will come. That's definite. Letting God have his way is the way to build your house on the solid rock instead of on the sand. The best time to make the decision to give God the chance is now. Give him the chance in issues of dating, choosing who to marry, conducting your courtship, and other important issues in marriage and life. In the words of one of the wisest men who ever lived on earth:

> *Remember your Creator*
> *in the days of your youth,*
> *before the days of trouble come.*
>
> Ecc 12:1 NIV

We have discussed knowing yourself. We have considered the concept of God as the author of marriage. We are acutely aware that some may not agree with our assertions about God. Again, we ask that the reader assume the concepts are true for now. Part of the puzzle is the question 'How can I allow God, especially if I do not know God?'

I met a young man, a more junior doctor, while I was in training. We got talking one evening when the shift was not busy. I asked his views on marriage. I was pleasantly surprised when he said that even though he was not religious, he was open to many views. One thing he said he could not fault Christianity on is her stance on marriage. I almost told him, as Jesus told the young ruler, that he was not far from the kingdom of God.

Even for a non-Christian, such assertions that God is the author of marriage make perfect sense. Many of us want the best from God. And we expect God to give us the best. Are we ready to allow God to give us the best in marriage? Would we go a step further and let him help us in other areas of life?

Many people are of the opinion that the Bible is archaic. Likewise, some people say that Shakespeare's plays are archaic.

It is a manifestation of ignorance in both cases. The Bible and Shakespeare's plays are alive to the people who are familiar with them. (I am in no way equating the two. I am only drawing an analogy.)

The principles discussed in this book are inspired by the Bible. Beyond marital bliss, the Author of marriage is waiting to give the whole of your life a brand-new meaning.

Allow God to help. He is always there to help. He says: 'Here I am! I stand at the door and knock. If anyone hears my voice and opens the door, I will come in and eat with that person, and they with me. (Revelation 3:20 NIV) For the reader who do not know where to start, a Bible and a Bible-believing church are recommended.

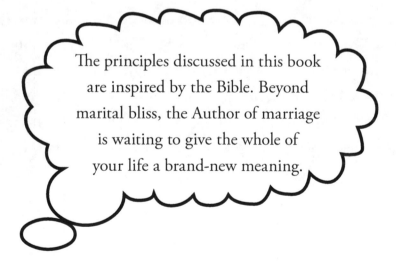

Chapter 11 Reflection

1. Find five passages in this book that support the idea of God's interest in marriage

———————————————————————————

———————————————————————————

———————————————————————————

———————————————————————————

———————————————————————————

CHAPTER 12

Can I prepare for sex?

Kunle

I will prepare and some day my chance will come."

— **Abraham Lincoln**

I remember when I got interested in sex. I had read a few books on marriage. One of the pages I turned to while skimming a book was about sex. Twenty-five years on, I remember the chapter started with 'I have a sneaking hunch this is one of the chapters you are reading first.'

Yes, in this time and age, the media bombards us with sexy images. Adverts scream sex. Businesses have adopted the slogan 'Sex sells!' Research shows that many problems in marriage are related to sex. It is therefore natural that readers will have a lot of questions about how to prepare for sex.

We sincerely believe that the Bible is a guide in life. The Bible contains many warnings about sex that was not engaged in the proper setting. The story of David and Bathsheba, for example, tells us about the dangers of unbridled sexual desires and actions.

It is interesting to find that many passages in the Bible talk positively about sex. The uninitiated reader may be pleasantly surprised, at this. It is most likely that the average person thinks the Bible only condemns sex. For example, the Bible tells us that Isaac lost his mother shortly before he married Rebecca, and experienced great comfort after going in unto Rebecca. As another example, the Song of Songs continues to inspire, challenge, and instruct couples about romance and fire their imaginations.

Understanding sexual union

As a junior doctor, when I was asked to list the organs involved in sex, my mind quickly jumped to anatomy class. Sexual organs? I came up with vulva, vagina, ovaries, and fallopian tubes for a woman, while for a man, Testicles, penis, scrotum, prostate were mentioned. I was pleasantly surprised to learn that the skin and the brain are considered among the organs involved in sex.

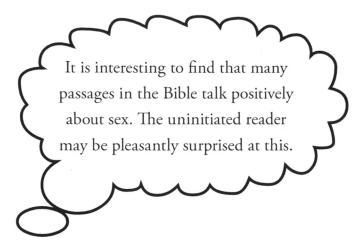

It is interesting to find that many passages in the Bible talk positively about sex. The uninitiated reader may be pleasantly surprised at this.

Sex, sexual union, and sexual fulfilment, like the simple illustration of sexual organs above, are easily and commonly misconstrued. It takes the whole being—spirit, soul, and body— to participate if sex is to be enjoyed fully. That sheds some light on the Judeo-Christian stance that when people have sex, it involves union. Paul says, 'Do you not know that he who unites himself with a prostitute is one with her in body? For it is said, "The two will become one flesh" (1 Cor 6:16 NIV).

Sex is not dirty

Almost by nature, people don't talk much about sex in the family. It is the advertisement industry that capitalises so much on the appeal of sex to our imaginations, thereby cashing in on our desires. Traditionally parents hardly talk to their children about sex.

I am a parent as well as a gynaecologist. I have been involved in couples' enrichment activities over the years, and I am comfortable talking about sex to couples. It is difficult, however, to discuss sex with my children. Difficult, but not impossible—it has to be done.

Because of parental challenges, children find out about sex from other sources. It is therefore common for some people to believe that sex is dirty. Well, if a lady is told for the first two decades of her life to keep her legs tightly closed (which is all the sexual education some receive), one can well imagine what effort and time it takes for some couples, even after marriage, to persuade the woman to keep her thighs open.

Sex is beautiful. It is God-given. When a couple wait for the right time, which is in marriage, sex is one of the most beautiful gifts of God.

Of course, some people have sex outside of marriage. It may be enjoyable, the same way Solomon testified that stolen water is sweet and bread eaten in secret is pleasant. But Solomon quickly added that the thief does not know that the dead are there too.

Sex is highly rated

As a gynaecologist, I have dedicated my professional practice to 'womanity'. Many complaints or conditions in my speciality directly interfere with sexual intercourse. Having asked my clients about frequency of sexual intercourse so many times has brought some revelation.

The group that surprises me most are women who are not having sex because their male partners have medical illnesses. Of course, the magazines and sexualised material in the media hardly mention these. They lead us to believe that in marriage, it is sex on demand.

Many people go into marriage with an insatiable appetite for sex—expectations that are too high for any human being to meet.

Those sexual scenes in movies that show clothes being ripped off and strewn all over the house are depicting the exception, despite the claim that it's the rule. In marriage, there will be times of such mutual ecstasy, but not at all times.

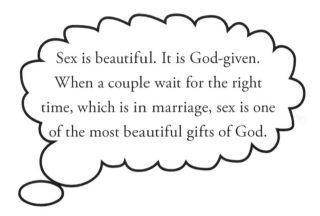

Sex is beautiful. It is God-given. When a couple wait for the right time, which is in marriage, sex is one of the most beautiful gifts of God.

The big picture

For the reader who lets his or her imagination run wild, it is important to consider that changes are inevitable in marriage. Marriage in itself is a time of tremendous adjustment. Leaving family and cleaving to a spouse has its challenges. Getting to know each other more intimately may unearth some surprises. And then there is pregnancy, whether planned or accidental or unachievable.

Therefore, preparation for sex should include a lot of mental preparation. You may marry a wife today who has accidents or go crazy tomorrow. This may be surprising and shocking, but it does happen to some people. Such should be an incentive for one to prepare one's mind for whatever marriage might throw at one.

Chapter 12 Reflection

1. What is your view on sex before marriage?

   _____

   _____

   _____

   _____

   _____

2. What are your expectations of sex in marriage?

   _____

   _____

   _____

   _____

   _____

CHAPTER 13

Pursue excellence

If you think education is costly, try ignorance.

Derek Bok

In public health, the association of poverty, ignorance, and disease is established. In similar manner, poverty and ignorance of the mind (which are still rampant in this information age) lead to disaster.

We have discovered, however, that information alone is not enough. We must painstakingly work through the issues raised. In this book we as authors have tried to raise issues we consider important in marriage, in order to sensitise the reader. It may suffice for some readers to take pen and paper and carry out self-assessment. Others may find it easier to discuss these issues with friends. The more you work through the issues that touch you, the better informed you will be.

We also recommend that the reader teach others. Teaching others affords the opportunity to chew over and digest the topic in question. Pitching the teaching to the right level for the audience helps your own grounding in the subject matter.

Lastly, being involved in issues of marriage not only enriches your life, but helps you to play your part in designing the kind of society you want to live in and want your children to live in. If you want to change the world, the best place to start is with yourself.

The pursuit of excellence, the quality of being outstanding, should not only be reserved for the professional realm. The world is getting tired of professionals who are excellent in their chosen fields but have marriages that do not reflect excellence.

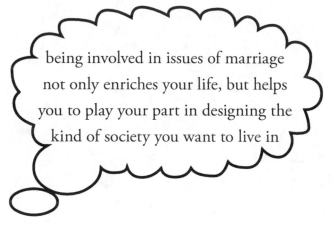

being involved in issues of marriage not only enriches your life, but helps you to play your part in designing the kind of society you want to live in

To pursue excellence in marriage and other aspects of life, we strongly recommend the principles discussed in this book. These principles helped us when we began our journey into the wonderful world of relationship, courtship, and marriage. There is no endeavour known to humanity where it has not been proven that preparation greatly increases the chances of success. Marriage is not exempt from this.

Don't settle for a penny. Don't settle for mediocrity in marriage. Do not leave your marriage to chance. Prepare.

Chapter 13 Reflections

1. What does it mean to you to pursue excellence in preparation for marriage?

_____

_____

_____

_____

_____

_____

_____

_____

_____

_____

2. How would you ensure you pursue excellence in marriage?

_____

_____

_____

_____

_____

_____

_____

_____

_____

_____

Printed in the United States
By Bookmasters